The Fingernail of Luck

Poems by Conrad Hilberry

The Fingernail of Luck

Poems by Conrad Hilberry

for Nancy and Jesse,
the best of friends over
all these years,
with love
from Con & Marion

Mayapple Press 2005

Published by   MAYAPPLE PRESS
408 N. Lincoln St.
Bay City, MI 48708
www.mayapplepress.com

ISBN 0-932412-33-5

ACKNOWLEDGMENTS:
Thanks to the journals that have published some of these poems: *Beloit Poetry Journal*: "Cherry Pie," "Deaf Ear," and "Waning Moon"; *Chautauqua Literary Journal*: "Oboe"; *Hudson Review*: "Alarm Clock," "Mouse-trap," and "Poker."

Cover photo of Conrad Hilberry by Anthony James Dougal

Cover and book design by Judith Kerman; typeset by Judith Kerman in Palatino text; all titles in Viner Hand ITC, cover text in Helvetica.

Contents

The Fingernail of Luck

Oboe

Your lips move moist around
my double reed, and I feel
the sad wind rising

through your throat. Some child
of yours is lost. If I were your
psychiatrist, I'd listen,

nod, prescribe. Instead,
I take your breath, shape it, let it find
a passage down this wooden

shaft, curl out around the ankles
of the clarinet. The horns
have forged a monumental

fountain on the stage and now
the strings supply the water,
surging up, looping, falling in

great sobs. The audience is weeping,
but you and I have doubts.
We wind our fiber through

the latticework of their grand art,
hoping someone may hear
the muscled twist

of grief that's seasoned
in a narrow tube, the hollow
music of a long-held breath.

Egg

You pass me from palm
to palm, run your eye along
my effortless asymmetry.

You handle me, knowing
my chalky curves
were turned on a lathe

of light. Palm to palm.
Before you make the next
move, do I remind you

of another yolk wrapped
in fragile bone, shapely,
golden in the center?

Do you recall how easily
a form you held
can crack and spill,

how absolute the absence?

Poker

Tongs open up into a laugh, remembering
they caught the live coal
in their jaws when Prometheus

first tossed it down. Somewhere they
roast an ox, heap up the fire.
And me? For a while I poked some logs.

Now I slouch here in the corner
watching the cabin give itself
to squirrels and roaches. The spider

I think of as my soul
climbs the cold chimney pipe,
finds it tarred at the roof, spins out

a line, and drops back down. That's
my spiritual adventure.
You might think the boys

in some back room would honor me
when they deal out their pairs
and flushes. I could suggest a ritual:

whenever a hand goes *straight*,
they might think of me, the unbent iron.
They might take off their hats.

No chance. I'm dust and ashes.
Rust. If I could find my heart
I'd pierce it, run it through.

Clue

Toffee with tooth marks, the petal
of hibiscus that never blooms
this far north, a scrap of toenail,

those are my cousins. I'm the left-handed
slash here on your kitchen door,
the stroke that missed, before you

sank the knife and caught your breath
there at the sink, your blouse
splattered with good riddance.

Believe me, I'm not blowing
any whistles. We've been acquainted
only since last Friday, but I can

feel some new air edging in
around your bed, your kitchen table.
The cabin settles into sumac

and the dog sleeps. Another clue
might roll its eyes
or lean a little toward the camera.

Not me. I'm just a slash
in old paint. If homicide shows up,
I'll drape a spider web

across my loin. But I'll be here,
the child of rage, your child.
Touch my deep diagonal, leftover

lightning. Follow my falling line
into the larger dark.
Even the bitterest rain

can sink into sand, collect in
the crevasses of rock, and lose
itself in the river's

lurch and surge and pause.

Passenger-Side Mirror

I glance over my shoulder,
a plainclothesman
letting you know what's lurking.

But you prefer to look
ahead, one hand on the wheel,
taking that curve below

the carved-out rock, moving in
whatever lane you choose.
You think a mirror's function

is to let you see the day receding,
everything you've crossed
or skirted diminishing behind you—

the flag girl there
in the construction zone, the slanted
Citroen easing toward its exit.

*Objects in mirror. . . .*You ignore
my messages. Remember
that school bus you passed? It's

not far behind us, five children's faces
in the windshield. And the smoking
pickup? It never did turn off.

While you've been terracing
the hills and parceling out
the bottomland, I've watched it

coming on, this huge blue fender,
inches from my face.

Cherry Pie

We're all acquainted with the airy
crowd—a stalk of celery dipped
in cottage cheese, a thimble

of soy milk, a few green grapes.
I invite them over here: between
two butter crusts, my sour

flesh so deeply sugared it
astounds the mouth.
To coax it all to bed, a downy

pillow of whipped cream.
Try me, you organics.
Light the oven.

Let me show you how
the juices leap, when nature
shares the sheets with art.

Quatrain

There's villanelle walking around,
retreating, a small bell echoing on
each ankle. Perched on the power line
are seven haikus, introspective, wan,

each one remembering a certain
cherry tree or golden carp
or thread of water down a rock.
And there's sestina in the park

shelling peanuts for her six
tame squirrels—each one takes a nut
and stays for her next stanza. Tall
in the evening light stands sonnet

under the courthouse pillars, fourteen
steps above the street. Me,
I never settled down. I rattle
on through town, waving to Bonnie

Barbara Allan, my old acquaintance,
still alive, pacing the graveyard.
My track curves below the free-verse
runnels, each one trying hard

to be a river. My wheels clack
over the ties, the rusting rails.
I take it slow, knowing I'm crammed
with crates of paint and pistols, bales

of fodder, motors that breathe oxygen
and oil. I am a box hitched
to a box hitched to a box, snaking
across the territory, switched

off the main line, bridging, tunneling,
turning up. I see the dock
and depot waiting to take me in.
They forget: I'm rolling stock.

Moustache

Hair up on top is white, but I'm
as dark as thirty—
a relic, a reminder. Eyes,

cheeks, and the other hangers-on
are in decline. Only
words have kept their resonance.

So, words, remember I'm
the formal awning under which
you signal for a cab,

the well-trimmed doorman, bowing
slightly, ushering you out.
If things go well, I'll look on

as your slippery diphthongs
warm the room, as you tuck
a metaphor in among the shrimp

and grape leaves. I like
the way you stroke me with your
consonants, but before

the evening's gone, you'll slip
back to stories
from another neighborhood

where once, in church,
you threw yourself away
and spoke in tongues. I wish

I'd known you then, your open
vowels and silences,
the ledge of your bare lips.

Alarm Clock

I'm here, indoor cricket
clicking you to sleep. Our pulses,
sixty even, straighten out the night.

I wake you—four quick beeps—
though I'd rather watch you
roll and mutter through some urgent

dream. Your thank-you
is to blip me on the head, male
hormones coming on at dawn

out of some ancient cave.
Evolution has its say, I guess.
I forgive you that. I know we're

different species, but I can't resist,
I keep offering my open face,
my nightly whisper

by your unshaved cheek.
No luck. That woman slips
under your sheet, and I

ache here on the windowsill.
I know I should hunt out
a mate of my own kind—

your shaver, maybe.
I can't do it. I'm cursed
with an unnatural affection.

Runoff

Hopeless weekends dripping
from the sky, notarized
lies, winged seeds, the arm

and eyelid of a doll—all this
is me, sloshing, taking my time—
bones of the banker rolled

in a green wind. Pablo Neruda,
my uncle, pours his sexual
water in my cracked cup. *Ruido*

rojo de huesos. Beetles roll
to the inhale of my blood—
whatever seeps from the lungs

of leaning houses, what percolates,
what shouts, what hugs the broken
post of its love. In a bad time,

when you're choking on smart
bombs and stupid ones,
I'm here to reassure you.

Aceite sin nombre. Your steel
towers, horn concertos,
blizzards, hairdos, sirens,

poems, palms, CD's, DVD's
SUV's—that's my lineage,
sloping down. Rain falls,

cracked clouds spill their
guttered news,
I take it all in my arms.

Hunch

Never mind the safe municipal
that claims to offer 3.8%
for fifteen years. Forget

the charts that promise you
the intracoastal channel
when the tide goes out. No

memorizing everything the deck
has dealt. Just follow me
into the tall grass swale

here by the woods. See the way
the sun gets broken
in that patch of swamp?

The way that droop of juniper
makes a doorway
to the dark? Soon you'll hear

the insects' smooth roulette
clicking out your name.
Inside this mound

I carry on my back, some ancient
bones are buried, a trove
where low life stirs,

where larval broods ferment
and generate. Put your hand here
where my humped shoulders

bend to the ground. Feel
the current? That's the fingernail
of luck, crawling up your arm.

Negative Space

Where the body isn't—that's how
dancers know me. Sculptors bend
their clay and steel against

my emptiness. Somehow, though I'm
not giving it a thought, I nudge
a shadow from a twist

of bronze or change the way
a breast and elbow size
each other up. Writers like to wrap

white space around their wit,
but I'm not white,
not bound or folded. I'm your

zero with its circumference
erased, an abandoned building
once the building's gone.   Let's say

a heavy childhood event
has bent your life, shaped
what you've become. Now you find

it never happened. Nothing
there at all. That's me.

Mousetrap

My parents were mousetraps
and my grandparents, an ancestry
of wood and wire. I knew my trade.

You should have seen me half
a century ago. Cocky. *Build a better
mousetrap,* someone would say.

I'd look him in the eye. *Some things
are what they are,* I'd say.
Can you build a better guillotine?

The blade falls—gravity with an edge.
Want to try a circular saw?
That was the way I talked back then.

Now I waste here on the shelf
behind the d-CON. No offspring,
end of the line. Still, after midnight,

I can feel my wire go taut
against the headboard, my curled
hips ready. I wait,

pretend to sleep. When something chews
the cheese between my legs,
everything I've stored

breaks free. The job is done,
done right. I draw a breath, lean back,
sleep out the night.

Electric Collar

I'm the cop you've hired
to enforce your petty ordinance.
Whenever Jessie races

toward the street beyond
the planted wire, I have to shoot
these bolts of fire

to her throat. But I love
that six-month hound. All day, I rub
the soft hairs of her neck

and she murmurs news
of everything under the leaves
and on the wind. These shocks—

as if someone made you whip
your daughter for roller skating
in the park. I have a plan.

Tonight I'll burnish up my brass,
unwrap my arms from Jessie's neck,
and snake my way into your

jewelry box. While you're considering
an item to set off your blouse,
I'll curl my languid leather

underneath your hand.
You'll take me to your throat
a Gucci touch, discreetly

punk. Then we'll step out—
high fashion, night air cool and moist,
and the streetlight, waiting.

Small Gray Box with Three Wires

We've all seen bodies when
the brain is gone. I'm the opposite,
intelligence unplugged,

waiting on the basement shelf.
Something's staggering without me,
but I can't remember what.

I swapped the circuits, forked
the frequencies, didn't notice
what the arms and wheels

might be doing. Some machine
must miss me. But it means that I
become the latest species—

a free-ranging brain. I'll find out
what conspiracies may be
fermenting in your

cellar, what's folded in your
ferny fractals.   I'm the celestial
weasel sniffing out

black holes. Hello, whose are
those blurred pikes
and pixels? A collusion!

Messy but I pull them up,
stash the squinting evidence.
You need some proof?

Here, Spade, I'll show you
where to dig, once I get my
glockles on the grid.

Deaf Ear

I watch a motorcycle smoking
on the street, tree tops wrestling,
some soprano hollowing

her arms and breasts and lips
around a body on the stage—
and, with them, no sound,

whatever that may be.
Mostly, I'm content. Seeing
is enough. But now I'm walking

a Nebraska road, at dawn,
before the cars have found it.
Over there, a square white house,

two pines, a shed and silo.
Four cows sleep in an endless
field. A full moon settles

west beyond a stand of timber,
and along a disappearing
line of fence, a dogwood

eases into bloom.
I see and breathe. No single
smell drifts in, but still

I take the scent of prairie
absences. Now I believe:
another door could open

on this emptiness. I long for it,
your huge countryside of silence.

Waning Moon

I rise at midnight when the first
sleep staggers into dream.
Later and lesser. In a week

I become the dark.
My music knows its way
to a Nash rusting by a shed,

the slow mating of snakes
in the creek bed. My half-moon
blues, my strum on the two

lanes of an empty road—
the road you're following
beside some dusty milkweed

and the fence. I draw my bow
across the telephone wires,
a thin dirge

for your nation, for the end
of something wild,
broad backed, generous.

Listen for me. With help
from the wind, I can pour
my six pale notes

through the night's sieve,
lend you the crickets' cadence
to walk home by.

Biographical Note

Conrad Hilberry is the author of nine previous collections of poetry, including *Player Piano*, *Sorting the Smoke: New and Selected Poems*, and *The Moon Seen as a Slice of Pineapple.* He lives in Kalamazoo, Michigan.

Other books from Mayapple Press

Margo Solod, *Some Very Soft Days,* 2005
    Paper, 84 pp, $15.50 plus s&h
    ISBN 0-932412-32-7
John Palen, *Open Communion,* 2005
    Paper, 98 pp, $16 plus s&h
    ISBN 0-932412-31-9
Susan Azar Porterfield, *In the Garden of Our Spines,* 2004
    Paper, 54 pp, $12.50 plus s&h
    ISBN 0-932412-30-0
Betsy Johnson, *What a Mouth Will Do,* 2004
    Paper, 36 pp, $8.50 plus s&h
    ISBN 0-932412-29-7
Martin Achatz, *The Mysteries of the Rosary,* 2004
    Paper, 62 pp, $10 plus s&h
    ISBN 0-932412-28-9
John Repp, *White Doe,* 2004
    Paper, 32 pp, $8.50 plus s&h
    ISBN 0-932412-27-0
Dennis Hinrichsen, *Message to Be Spoken into the Left Ear of God,* 2004
    Paper, 52 pp, $8.50 plus s&h
    ISBN 0-932412-26-2
Johnny Durán, *Nieblas de Luna/Moon Fogs,* 2004
    Paper, 52 pp, $8.50 plus s&h
    ISBN 0-932412-23-8
Adrienne Lewis, *Coming Clean,* 2003
    Paper, 30 pp, $8 plus s&h
    ISBN 0-932412-21-1
Pamela Miller, *Recipe for Disaster,* 2003
    Paper, 66 pp, $12 plus s&h
    ISBN 0-932412-19-X
Gerry LaFemina, *Zarathustra in Love,* 2001
    Paper, 44 pp, $8.50 plus s&h
    ISBN 0-932412-18-1
Judith Kerman and Don Riggs, eds.,
Uncommonplaces: Poems of the Fantastic, 2000
    Paper, 148 pp, $15 plus s&h
    ISBN 0-932412-17-3
Poems by leading s.f. and fantasy authors, including
Brian Aldiss, Joe Haldeman, Jeanne Larsen, David
Lunde, Patrick O'Leary, Rick Wilber, & Jane Yolen
Helen Ruggieri, *Glimmer Girls,* 1999
    Paper, 40 pp, $8 plus s&h
    ISBN 0-932412-16-5
Zack Rogow, *The Selfsame Planet,* 1999
    Paper, 40 pp, $7.50 plus s&h
    ISBN 0-932412-15-7

Larry Levy, *I Would Stay Forever If I Could,* 1999
Paper, 36 pp, $6.50 plus s&h
ISBN 0-932412-14-9
Skip Renker, *Sifting the Visible,* 1998
Paper, 36 pp, $6.50 plus s&h
ISBN 0-932412-13-0
Hugh Fox, *Strata,* 1998
Paper, 28 pp, $5.50 plus s&h
ISBN 0-932412-12-2
John Palen, *Staying Intact,* 1997
Paper, 28 pp, $6 plus s&h
ISBN 0-932412-11-4
Judith McCombs, *Territories, Here & Elsewhere,* 1996
Paper, 28 pp, $6 plus s&h
ISBN 0-932412-10-6
Kip Zegers, *The American Floor,* 1996
Paper, 24 pp, $6 plus s&h
ISBN 0-932412-09-2
Al Hellus, *a vision of corrected history with breakfast,* 1995
Paper, 24 pp, $5 plus s&h
ISBN 0-932412-08-4
David Lunde, *Blues for Port City,* 1995
Paper, 24 pp, $5 plus s&h
ISBN 0-932412-07-8
Evelyn Wexler, *Occupied Territory,* 1994
Paper, 80 pp, $10 plus s&h
ISBN 0-932412-06-8
Evelyn Wexler, *The Geisha House,* 1992
Paper, 24 pp, $5.50 plus s&h
ISBN 0-932412-05-X
Judith Minty, *Letters to my Daughters,* 1981
Paper, 24 pp, $5 plus s&h
ISBN 0-932412-04-3
Toni Ortner-Zimmerman,
As If Anything Could Grow Back Perfect, 1979
Paper, 16 pp, $5 plus s&h
ISBN 0-932412-02-5

Also available through Mayapple Press:
Judith Kerman, *Plane Surfaces/Plano de Incidencia,* 2002,
CCLEH
Bilingual, translations by Johnny Durán
Paper, 144 pp, $15 plus s&h
ISBN 0-932412-20-3
Dulce María Loynaz, *La Carta de Amor al Rey Tut-Ank-Amen/The Love Letter to King Tutankhamen,* 2002, CCLEH
Bilingual, translation by Judith Kerman.
Limited edition of 250, signed & numbered.
Paper, 28 pp, $10 plus s&h
ISBN 0-932412-24-6

Judith Kerman, *Mothering & Dream of Rain,* 1996,
Ridgeway Press
 Paper, 88 pp, $12 plus s&h
 ISBN 0-932412-22-X
Judith Kerman, *3 Marbles,* 1999, Cranberry Tree
 Paper, 32 pp, $7 plus s&h
 ISBN 0-9684218-1-4
Judith Kerman, *Driving for Yellow Cab,* 1985, Tout
Press
 Paper, 16 pp, $5 plus s&h
 ISBN 0-932412-04-1

Sample poems and the latest information for all
Mayapple Press publications are available online at
www.mayapplepress.com